AFFIRMING

Ross Thompson

IS THERE AN ANGLICAN WAY?

Scripture, Church and Reason:
New Approaches to an Old Triad

Series Editor: Jeffrey John

DARTON·LONGMAN+TODD

First published in 1997 by
Darton, Longman and Todd Ltd
1 Spencer Court
140–142 Wandsworth High Street
London SW18 4JJ

in association with

Affirming Catholicism
St Giles Church
No 4, The Postern
Wood Street, The Barbican
London EC2Y 8BJ

© 1997 Ross Thompson

ISBN 0–232–52221–9

The views expressed in this booklet are those of the
author and do not necessarily reflect any policy
of Affirming Catholicism

Designed by Bet Ayer
Phototypeset by Intype London Ltd
Printed and bound in Great Britain by
Page Bros, Norwich

Affirming Catholicism

Affirming Catholicism is a movement (not an ecclesiastical party) which exists to do two things. We affirm our confidence in our Anglican heritage; and we seek to renew and promote the Catholic tradition within it. Our aim is to explore, explain and share with others both inside and outside the Church a lively, intelligent and inclusive Catholic faith. In the words of our Trust Deed:

> It is the conviction of many that a respect for scholarship and free enquiry has been characteristic of the Church of England and of the Churches of the wider Anglican Communion from earliest times, and is fully consistent with the status of those Churches as part of the Holy Catholic Church. It is desired to establish a charitable educational foundation which will be true both to those characteristics and to the Catholic tradition within Anglicanism ... The object of the foundation shall be the advancement of education in the doctrines and the historical development of the Church of England and the Churches of the wider Anglican Communion, as held by those standing within the Catholic tradition.

Our Publications

These are offered as one means of presenting Anglican Catholic teaching and practice in as clear and accessible a form as possible. Some cover traditional doctrinal and liturgical themes; others attempt to present a well-argued Catholic viewpoint on issues of debate currently facing the Church. There are a list of our series of booklets on page v.

The present series of books is provided, where appropriate, with summaries to sections, and suggested questions which we hope will facilitate personal study or discussion in groups. Other titles in the series are:

The Ministry of Deliverance Dominic Walker OGS
By What Authority? – Authority, Ministry and the Catholic Church Mark D. Chapman
Marriage, Divorce and the Church Anthony Harvey

To order these publications individually or on subscription, or for further information about the aims and activities of Affirming Catholicism, write to:

The Secretary
Affirming Catholicism
St Giles Church
No 4, The Postern
Wood St
Barbican
London EC2Y 8BJ

Tel 0171 638 1980
Fax 0171 638 1997

Booklets in the Affirming Catholicism series

Affirming Confession John Davies

Catholicism and Folk Religion Jeremy Morris

Christ in Ten Thousand Places – A Catholic Perspective on Christian Encounter with Other Faiths Michael Ipgrave

History, Tradition and Change – Church History and the Development of Doctrine Peter Hinchliff

Imagining Jesus – An Introduction to the Incarnation Lewis Ayres

'Is the Anglican Church Catholic?' – The Catholicity of Anglicanism Vincent Strudwick

Lay Presidency at the Eucharist Benedict Green

'Making Present' – The Practice of Catholic Life and Liturgy Christopher Irvine

'Permanent, Faithful, Stable' – Christian Same-Sex Partnerships Jeffrey John

Politics and the Faith Today – Catholic Social Vision for the 1990s Kenneth Leech

Trinity and Unity Jane Williams

What is Affirming Catholicism? Jeffrey John

Why Women Priests? – The Ordination of Women and the Apostolic Ministry Jonathan Sedgwick

About the Author

Ross Thompson is currently vicar of St Barnabas and Holy Cross in the U. P. A. parish of Knowle West, Bristol, where he works alongside his wife and two other colleagues.

His writings include *Holy Ground, the Spirituality of Matter*, and he continues to write and teach in his present setting. He is the clergy representative for Bristol Diocese on the General Council of Affirming Catholicism.

Contents

Introduction   1
Are Anglicans lost?   3
The Anglican Triad   4
Doing without 'basics'   6
Summary   9

Scripture: The Inbreathed Word   10
Summary   14

Church: Organism, Assembly and
Communion   16
Models of unity   16
The Church: organism, crystal or fractal?   20
How God's Word informs the Church   23
Tradition and communion   27
Summary   29

Reason: Contemplative Imagination   31
Summary   34

Prospects   36
Summary   42

Questions   43

Notes and References   48

IS THERE
AN ANGLICAN WAY?

Introduction

In those computer adventure games that are one of the uncovenanted blessings of modern vicarage life, the computer is wont to announce things like: 'The path ahead leads through a dark, narrow defile. What now?' Let us imagine that the players in the great Adventure Game of the Anglican Church confront just such a decision as to what to do and where to go. As they survey the forbidding scene before them, the travellers in the group are divided. Some think the group should press on, others think the main path is that faint looking one that climbs up the side of the rocks, avoiding the dangerous river in the heart of the defile, while yet others begin to think that the group has been coming the wrong way for quite some time, and needs to turn round and troop back to safer territory and better trodden paths.

Determining the right path ought to be easy, but unfortunately, does not prove so. Some have taken out their compasses and are busy taking bearings. They have brand new, up-to-date, precision models which, they insist, are completely sufficient for the task, so they refuse even a glance at the 2000-year-old maps over which others are busy poring. The map people, meanwhile, regard these new-fangled devices as dangerous, unreliable innovations, and urge that the maps, old as they are, contain all things necessary to finding the way. A third party proposes that in cases of dispute like this, the leader should arbitrate. After all, he is an experienced explorer who knows this territory like the back of his hand and has made deep study of the accounts of previous explorers. He does not need maps and compasses and other artificial aids; if only everyone would accept the cumulative weight of experience he represents, all would be well. But to the others, this view seems to give too much weight to human authority. The dispute rages on, as daylight fades.

As if this were not confusion enough, the maps have no key to the symbols on them, so what could be meant to be a great immovable mountain could, after all, be an impenetrable forest, and what some insist is the smooth highway that connects everything, others take to be a treacherous backwater. Moreover, the strict map-people say that the blank areas on the map must correspond to actual deserts where it would be foolish to venture, while others argue that they just represent the areas the map-makers never explored, but which may contain the most fertile land of all. At this point the compass people intervene, suggesting they could take bearings to see what the maps refer to on the ground, but the map people will not have their all-sufficient maps questioned by upstart modernist methods. So the map-folk disintegrate into a melée of warring map-factions, each battling for their own interpretation of the map.

It is nearly dark now and the party finally takes a vote, in which it is decided to press on down the defile. The majority – a mixture of all three parties, leader included – march on. But some of the leader-folk argue that this leader has compromised himself, and troop off towards the safer ground in search of a rumoured 'true' leader. Others among the map-folk stand on the higher ground urging the majority to repent and turn back. And yet another group argues on fashionable philosophical grounds that the maps are not meant to relate to the land anyway, and there is no right path; they sit down right where they are and start meditating on the mandala-like patterns on the 'maps', and contemplating the breathtaking light of the setting sun reflected in their compasses.

Are Anglicans lost?

Is this a fair picture of the Anglican Church? No doubt the reader will have discerned ways of interpreting my little allegory. The defile could be the ordination of women; though other issues (sexual morality; lay presidency; liturgical reform...) provoke similar confusion. The map-folk are the Evangelicals who look to the Bible, the compass-folk are the Liberals who look to the guiding light of reason and up-to-date insight – something we each possess, but need to polish and bring up to date – while the leader-folk are the Catholics who look for consensus and continuity among the faithful of the Church, and in case of dispute, resort to magisterial authority. The trickle going back to the well-trodden ways is of course Forward in Faith, the hecklers on the high ground are Reform, and the contemplatives Don Cupitt's Sea of Faith group.

So is the Anglican Communion as well and truly lost as the sad little party in my story? Can the taking of a vote on General Synod be compared with the explorers' desperate vote? On the face of it, there is plenty of ground for pessimism here. We go on and on asking the wrong question. We ask, which faction is going the right way? Which faction has the right approach? And that is a question that perpetuates our state of being lost.

For the real sadness of the story is that between them the explorers have everything they need to find the way. My pessimism about Anglicanism stems from, and gains the urgency of its frustration from, a root optimism, to the effect that we are blessed with a balance of the tools we need. We simply need to change the question, and ask, how should maps be used in conjunction with compasses? And what is the place for the leader, and for the solid experience he represents, of those who have long trodden this kind of territory? How can we correlate our slightly different biblical maps with the rooted experience of tradition and the compass of modern insight, so that we know where we have been, where we are, and where we need to go?

The Anglican Triad
The basic tools I have allegorised in map, compass, and experience of terrain represent, of course, the triad affirmed as the basis of Anglican authority since Richard Hooker: Scripture, reason and Church

tradition.[1]* But simply to say that these are needed in a certain balance is no more helpful than to tell an expedition to use a balanced combination of the map, the compass, and the leader's expert authority! It is precisely the art of using the three together that matters, and that, as a communion, we have perhaps yet fully to learn. Aidan Nichols is probably right to argue, in his valuable critique, *The Panther and the Hind*,[2] that Anglicanism has often represented the kind of 'trialogue of the deaf' I have just satirised.

Nicholls' own solution, however, is submission to a universally recognised *magisterium* with authority to adjudicate between the three voices and decide as to truth. This reflects his Roman Catholic position, and represents a decisive step into one of the three camps: that for which the Church is the supreme – or at least, the decisive – authority. And that brings us to our central problem: the way each authority has something absolute about it. The Church possesses a tendency to wield absolute institutional authority. But the Bible, if it is divine revelation, must needs be the final arbiter of all claims. Yet equally, since Descartes, reason tends to subject all claims but its own to radical doubt, so as to retain only that we can be absolutely sure of. (The 'spectrum' view, which identifies the liberals as tolerant Broad Church people in the true centre of Anglicanism, ignores the fact that liberals, too, can be hardline and thoughtlessly dismissive of opponents.[3]) In this tradition Kant argued that reason

*For notes and references see p. 48.

and conscience need to set even the claims of Christ before their own tribunal.

How then can there be peace between such absolute powers? How can the Anglican triad begin to function? The decisive step is to examine what makes the three make their claims so absolute. Is absolutism the only way of doing the claims justice? Or is there really something as absurd about such absolutism as there is about those who make absolute claims for map, leader or compass?

Doing without 'basics'

It turns out, I suggest, that Scripture, reason and tradition are necessary *rivals only within what I term foundationalism*, rivals within the characteristically modern enterprise of building knowledge on certainty.[4] 'Foundationalism' is not quite fundamentalism. Fundamentalism sticks to what it sees as the basics and forbids us to go beyond them in any way. Foundationalism allows us to build on the basics, and restricts us only to what can be firmly established solely on their basis. Fundamentalism, to caricature a little, requires us to live in the foundations of the house; foundationalism allows us to build a house on the foundations, but won't allow us to extend the house, still less to build bridges across chasms to other houses with different foundations. Both foundationalism and fundamentalism agree, however, that foundations are crucial and 'unfounded' imaginative chasm-leaping bridges are out of the question. Both picture truth as a journey with a totally dependable starting point, reversing a more traditional Christian view that justifies the truth-journey in terms of its totally dependable goal in God. For traditional Christianity, absolute assurance is eschatological – something we reach only in the 'end-time' – an affair of faith, hope and love in the meantime.

But both fundamentalism and foundationalism are opposed to the process I am advancing, for which there are no universally obvious risk-free starting points in our knowledge of God, but that knowledge is rather something we discover 'on the way' in the process of living the Church, engaging in dialogue with the Scriptures, and reflecting imaginatively upon the contemporary world around us, as we proceed, never leaving that world behind, towards a horizon of assurance we can never in this life cross.

So it is the same error that leads the Protestant to seek certainty in Scripture alone, and the Catholic to seek it in Church structures alone, and the liberal to seek it by the rational method of doubt. In each case we look for truth in terms of proof from unquestionable foundations. But science after Polanyi and Kuhn, and even mathematics after Gödel, have had to admit that the true is larger than the provable: we will never be able to be sure of all the facts (see footnote 4). The search for proven certainty is as much a distraction, indeed an absurdity, in ethics, in theology, or in science, as it is in the case of our expedition. The expedition does not need to know for certain the exact detail of the terrain, or to be able to prove which path is right; it needs only to be able to decide which path is most likely to be profitable in furthering the journey. And it has all it needs for that.

Likewise, theologically, 'we walk by faith, not by sight' (2 Cor. 5:7). Or as Henry Vaughan put it, laying bare a mystical undercurrent in Anglicanism:

> There is in God, some say
> A deep, but dazzling darkness; As men here
> Say it is late and dusky, because they
> See not all clear.[5]

Those who depart and walk with us no longer almost invariably pose the question as one of *authority*. That poses it in an un-Anglican way that already predisposes us to an un-Anglican answer. It supposes that the basic question is that of giving sure foundations for what one believes and sure justification for what one does. But this is the wrong question, not only, as just argued, methodologically, but also theologically! We are justified not by our own infallible writings, institutions or arguments, but by God alone, through faith. We can never 'prove' that we are doing right. The question is rather one of *integrity*: whether, through what a church does, the dazzling darkness of Christ authentically shines. If it does not so shine, then however loud and clear its attempts to justify itself, that church has lost its soul, ceased to be Church.

Within Anglicanism lie, I think, a view of the Church that is un-Roman but as positive as the Roman Catholic, a view of the Bible that is un-biblicist but thoroughly biblical, and a view of reason that is un-secular yet more positive than the secular. It is the powerful non-absolutism that Anglicanism ascribes to all three that allows them to interact without any of them being supreme arbiter.

Summary
Many think that the Anglican Church has 'lost its way'. The differences between the various ideological tendencies within the Anglican mix show up particularly in face of controversial current questions about, for example, the ordination of women or same-sex relationships. The three main groups in these debates roughly correspond to the well-known triad of Scripture, tradition and reason, and so these sources of authority can often come to be seen in opposition to each other, Evangelicals arguing for the primacy of Scripture, Liberals for the primacy of reason, and Catholics for the primacy of tradition and hierarchical authority.

But Scripture, tradition and reason are not rivals, or only appear so when an absolutist view is taken of one or the other. It is simply a mistake to seek infallible certainty in any one of the three. Infallibility belongs to God alone, not to Scripture, reason or tradition, and for the moment we live by faith. This means that we must not expect easy answers. True authority can only be sought, in faith and with integrity, from a considered weighing of the *interaction* of all three sources of authority, without any one of them being allowed to be the supreme arbiter.

Scripture: The Inbreathed Word

Consider the following extracts from the Articles of The Book of Common Prayer:

> Holy Scripture containeth all things necessary to salvation; so that whatsoever is not read therein, nor may be proved thereby, is not to be required of any man.
>
> *(Article VI)*

> The Church hath power to decree Rites and Ceremonies, and authority in Controversies of Faith: And yet it is not lawful for the Church to ordain any thing that is contrary to God's Word written.
>
> *(Article XX)*

Anglican tradition thus proclaims its faith in the Scriptures in a liberating manner, as a way of freeing us from those rules and constraints of the Church that go beyond what Scripture can justify. However, some conservative Evangelical groups such as Reform – which reflect a growing position within Anglicanism – go way beyond this. The move is made from the view of the Articles that there is nothing that *must* (for salvation) be believed that is not provable from Scripture, to what we may term the *biblicist* view that nothing may be believed that is contrary to Scripture, or the even stronger *fundamentalist* position that everything in Scripture must be believed – that Scripture is morally and factually infallible.

Biblicism, while not contrary to Scripture, is not a biblical view. The Word of God is certainly said in Scripture to be immutable, all powerful and infallible – witness Isaiah 40:8, 55:10–11 and the prophetic use of 'Thus says the Lord'. But both the Hebrew *dabar* and the Greek *logos*, which translate into our 'word', carry a variety of meanings. There is the *dabar*, the pre-eminently context-related and *spoken* Word of the prophets. There is the *logos*, the Johannine Word that is the reason and intelligibility behind the universe, dwelling as the light in everyone who comes into the world. Above all for Christians there is that Word made flesh in the human life of Jesus Christ.

From a genuinely biblical point of view, it is Christ alone who in the truest sense is the living and eternal Word of God. We have access to him *through* the word of Scripture, but he is not to be identified with it. We also have access to him through *the indwelling word* of reason whose incarnation he is, yet he is not to be identified with human reason either. And we have access to him through the Church, his continuing Body, and yet he is always greater than the Church. Christ the true and living Word comes to be known by us in these three ways: through the word of Scripture; through the indwelling reason of our humanity; and through the life of the Church – but he is not tied down by any of them. In fact, a truly biblical understanding of the Word leads not to biblicism but to something remarkably like the Anglican triad!

We might also note the way the three parts of the Old Testament correspond with something – bearing in mind the historical gulf – uncannily close to the triad. The *torah*, with its concern (expressed through the various layers of its editing) for the origins and stories of the patriarchs, for laws and traditions, for priesthood, liturgy and ritual holiness, corresponds with the Anglican emphasis on Church tradition; the prophets, speakers of a radical, authoritatively challenging Word, relate to the Evangelical stress on the Bible as something cleansing, renewing, demanding personal response and (in classical and recent Evangelicalism) making for justice; while the wisdom literature, with its more reflective, philosophical, urbane and often downright sceptical approach, suggests the liberal strand of Anglicanism.

Finally, the Bible is diverse not only in type, but in time: it is evolving and innovative. Jesus and Paul root what they have to say in the Hebrew Scriptures, but cannot be said to *prove* what they say from them. They say new things, and sometimes things that contradict those Scriptures (e.g. Matthew 5:31–2). Such contradiction is quite compatible with the fulfilment (*pleroma*, filling up, completion) of Scripture that Jesus speaks of in Matthew 5:17. Indeed, the Bible shows a story of fulfilment through contradiction, retelling and resolution. The prophets themselves spoke the Word of God, not by quoting tracts of the *torah* and applying them to 'current moral issues', but by retelling the Exodus in new ways that impacted on the present and unfolded into a future hope. Out of the interaction between *torah* and present time, new truths spilled, and new ethical visions, including the Messianic hope, emerged.[6]

But this is a process that continues in the Church. Once we see the Scriptures as 'God breathed' (*theópneustos*, 2 Timothy 3:16, the word for 'breathed' having connotations also of spirit, influence, breeze, wind) we will look for movement in the Bible. We will look not only to the way the biblical branches form a structure in which we can build the Church's nests, but also to the wind those branches' movement bears witness to, the wind on which we nestlings must learn to fly. (Precisely those movements that make things uncertain and shaky from a nesting point of view, carry us further when we fly!) And that breath or wind is not something we will expect to die; only if the Church goes on retelling the story in new ways can the biblical story be understood in our time. The biblical 'map' is obscure and has no key, except the spoken interpretation of those who over the centuries have been walking the land, and can hand down from lived experience what the enigmas on the map refer to.

For Anglicans the Bible is less a book to be read than speech to be breathed, proclaimed and sung – as doubtless much of it, as oral tradition, originally was. An Orthodox is likely to carry with her a visual 'word' in the icon; a Roman Catholic a means of prayer in the rosary; a Protestant the written word of the Bible; but for Anglicans the treasure in the pocket or handbag is most likely to be *The Book of*

Common Prayer, or these days perhaps *Celebrating Common Prayer* – the prayed Word. There is in Anglicanism, we note, no machinery for the direct development of doctrine, only for the development of its embodiment in the worshipping community, through the liturgy. Recent Anglican provision – in *Celebrating Common Prayer, Patterns for Worship, the Promise of his Glory* and so forth – provides a rich provision of God's Word as Canticle, as that which we tell and sing and weave into the day-to-day fibre of the worship of the Church. The Church is woven from the Word, and cannot be told apart from the Word, nor the Word apart from it. But what notion of the Church does this imply?

Summary
Anglican formularies relating to Scripture tell us that nothing has to be believed or done by Christians beyond what can be proved out of Scripture. In that sense the approach is open and positive. By contrast biblicism takes a restrictive approach, asserting nothing may be believed which is contrary to Scripture; and fundamentalism takes the still harder line that everything in Scripture must be believed, and that Scripture itself is morally and factually infallible.

The biblicist and fundamentalist tendency to equate the Word of God with the literal word of Scripture is untrue to what is said in Scripture itself, where the word is variously understood as: (1) The written or spoken word as literally recorded in Scripture; (2) the logos or reason inherent in God and shared with humanity, made incarnate in Jesus; (3) Jesus himself as the Word of God made flesh. In the truest sense the Word of God *is* Christ himself, who is made known to us through Scripture, through reason, and through the Church which is his continuing Body on earth; but who is to be equated with none of them. Rather we come to know Christ as the living Word only by the interaction between Scripture, reason, and Church as we seek to serve him in the present. Scripture itself is the product and record of the Spirit's action on the writers in their own time; but it is the Spirit in us who brings the written word alive and makes the living Word present to us now.

Church: Organism, Assembly and Communion

The issue here – how biblical truth is lived by, informs, and edifies the Church – hinges on the relation between the individual member with her or his personal faith and the corporate faith of the body of Christ. Exploring this relation will help explain some of the subtle differences between our churches, so I hope the ordinary reader will bear with some quite complex concepts here, just as the scientist or philosopher will bear with my simplifications, as we look, first, at some models of how parts may form a unifying whole.

Models of unity

• THE CRYSTAL. The beauty of a diamond, say, consists in its sheer transparent simplicity. Its structure and symmetry are entirely based on those of its constituent atoms and the way they bond together. A crystal grows in solution – in the way many of us remember from our childhood chemistry sets – as individual atoms or molecules bond on to the existing structure of atoms one by one. Reductionism holds true – the idea that the whole is no more than simply the sum of its constituent parts – and this gives to the whole its elemental and starkly powerful unity.

• THE ORGANISM. When more diverse parts are put together for a purpose that transcends them, according to a blueprint, we have a machine. In a sense the machine can be reduced to constituent parts – a car, for example, into engine and wheels and chassis and so forth – but then the machine itself no longer exists, because its function cannot be performed by the parts in isolation. The whole machine can, on the other hand, do many things no part can do in isolation. Some of these things will be a function contributed by a particular part – the engine, for instance, drives the car along – though this function could not be performed by the engine on its own! Other functions need the co-operation of several parts: steering, for instance, is performed by a combination of the various parts linking the steering wheel to the front wheels. But the main point is that though the machine consists of parts, it has properties that the parts in isolation do not. And the beauty of a machine consists in the way its individual parts co-ordinate efficiently to achieve the purpose of the whole. If a machine can organize and run its own actions – containing somehow within itself the blueprint that co-ordinates it – then we call it an organism.

• THE FRACTAL. Very often the pattern of clouds, especially in a mackerel sky, or say the patterns left by waves along a seashore, or larger scale weather patterns, show a self-organizing feature that has been given the name 'fractal', an infinitely complex pattern that exhibits an order we would not have expected just from the laws that govern the individual parts. The science to help us understand this kind of process is only now developing: recent complexity theory has studied the operation of what it terms *emergent* laws: where one might have expected the laws operating on individual atoms to have cancelled out and produced the random disorder of a cloud of dust or gas, in a mysterious way the atoms begin to co-ordinate as a whole revealing an unanticipated pattern, like the intricacy of a mackerel sky.

Whereas the machine is designed from the top down, as it were, the parts being chosen to fit into the whole functional design; and the crystal is formed from the bottom up, the pattern of atoms at bottom level determining the symmetry at the level we can see; the fractal is formed by an 'emergent' law that is neither imposed from above nor determined from below. The lower level – the actual atoms that make the fractal pattern up – can change completely while the top level – the fractal itself – remains: it is a pattern in which the atoms participate rather than a structure they permanently make up. Thus a cloud arising in high wind as moist air passes over a mountain retains its beautiful lens shape even though it is formed by an ever changing series of water molecules, and a flame may persist in an ever-changing flow of burning gas.[8]

• THE BODY. Here we have an organism that can not only organize but grow itself and reproduce itself. In a nutshell, bodies are complex crystals that grow into organisms by fractal means. As has been discovered, we grow out of the complex crystal that is the DNA molecule twisted into the heart of each of our cells, by means of a whole host of self-regulating and spontaneously self-organizing 'fractal' interactions, into an organism that functions coherently to achieve its own goals.

To sum up:

* As *growing* beings we are complex *crystals*. The whole of us is in some sense implicit in the DNA molecules in each cell of our body.

* As *living and conscious* beings we are *fractals*. As with the flame, our molecules change while we remain. We are spontaneously self-organizing, and though consciousness remains a mystery, it certainly cannot be identified with a function of any particular part of us, material or immaterial. There is, as William James urged, no 'pontifical neurone' through which the contents of the brain have to pass to become conscious. Modern theories model the mind rather as a society of cooperating and competing elements, gaining ascendancy in turn. Indeed, our thoughts seem to crystallize out of the flux of unconscious neuronal activity much in the same beautifully self-organizing way as the fractal patterns of clouds or waves on the shore. So consciousness relates to its contents as the flickering flame to the ever changing stream of molecules that fleetingly participate in its dance.[9]

* As *active, moving*, beings, we are *organisms*, beautifully co-ordinated to carry out the functions of life. Our parts are knit together in a tightly organized hierarchical flow of control, which brings information into the centre, the brain, and instructions regarding movement out, again, from that centre.

The Church: organism, crystal or fractal?

Most Christians would accept, as one main biblical analogy for the Church, that it is the Body of Christ (cf. 1 Corinthians 12, and throughout the writings of Paul). But different ways of looking at the way parts relate to the whole in the body will lead to diverse conceptions of the relation between the individual and the Church as a whole. I suggest the way the various churches live their lives correspond to the following understandings, partly explicit in doctrine, partly implicit in a church's practice.

• THE ROMAN CATHOLIC understanding views the Body of Christ as a supernatural *organism*, a body viewed as a centred hierarchy of control, a sublime machine divinely constructed to carry out the divine purpose in the world. The Roman Church, tightly focused on the Papal head, is admirably geared to move (fast when it needs to) from first principles to militant action in the world. Each part carries out, for the whole, a particular function, the *magisterium* for example playing a role in the whole Church's believing analogous to that of the eyes in the whole body's seeing. So Roman Catholic worship is the act of the whole Church, a process in which the various members – priests, servers, choir, readers, people – have distinctive parts to play as in a beautiful organism; not least the priest, who offers the Eucharist as the sacrifice of the whole body of Christ, focused in the moment of consecration.

• THE PROTESTANT view regards the Church as a *crystal*, that is, as something that grows out of the faith of its members. The pattern of the Body of Christ reflects the pattern of the Christ who indwells each true believer. The result is a reductionist approach to the Church, in the sense that whole Church is present in each member, just as the whole body is implicit in the DNA in each cell of the body, which controls how the body will grow. The faith, holiness and worship of the Church are brought to it by the individual members rather than being something that belongs first of all to the whole Church: the priesthood of the Church implies a primary priesthood of all its members, and decisions are made by all the members gathered together in their congregations. Protestant worship, like the crystal, is simple, transparent to God, the devotion of the individual writ large through multiple reflections in others gathered for worship. Hence the austere, didactic, memorial structure of the Protestant Last Supper; the richness is all inward, as the members feed on Christ by faith at the crucial moment of communion in which the institution narrative culminates.

• THE ANGLICAN approach, at least from Hooker onward, reveals (possibly with Eastern Orthodoxy) greater stress on the Church's *fractal*, self-organizing, emergent qualities like *koinonia* or communion.[10] These qualities are analogous to the life and the consciousness of the body: things each believer has potentially, but which are only realized through belonging to the whole, and which spill down from the whole to the parts. As every part of the cloud is still cloud, every part of the Church is still fully Church, so that it is doubtful whether we should ever properly talk of 'parts' of the Church at all. This is not, however, because the whole Christ is implicit in each individual believer, as with the Protestant 'crystal', but because the *koinonia* of the Church takes up every individual into a dance that transcends her and enables her to obey the 'emergent' divine law of love. So for Anglicans worship is 'common prayer' – a communion in prayer – and the Eucharist is not *primarily* either a corporate sacrifice or personal memorial (though it includes these dimensions) but Holy Communion, a real sharing in the divine life through the body of Christ.[11] By relocating Communion within the prayer of Consecration itself, straight after the institution narrative and before the prayer of oblation, Cranmer's Eucharist unites Consecration and Communion into a single act, conflating the crucial Catholic and Protestant moments. For the real presence that matters to Cranmer – as is clear from one of the alternative postcommunion prayers of oblation – is not the 'natural' presence consecrated on the altar, nor the subjective presence communed with in each believer's heart, but a movement of real participation in the heavenly Christ.[12] Christ is present in his *mystical* or *spiritual* body:

> We most heartily thank thee, for that thou dost vouchsafe to feed us, who have duly received these holy mysteries, with the spiritual food of the most precious body and blood of thy Son ... and that we are very members incorporate in the mystical body of thy Son.

How God's Word informs the Church

We are now in a position to see how these different understandings (often implicit rather than defined) of the body bear on our central issue: how the body of Christ finds its way in terms of faith. I will need to be brief and paint with a very broad brush. We note how the opposites of Protestantism and Catholicism converge in many ways, leaving Anglicanism (again bracketed with Eastern Orthodoxy here) as offering not a mere middle term but something distinctive over against them; something that, because it has yet to be fully explored theologically, has often been neglected.

• THE ROMAN CATHOLIC – at least, in the traditional, and now resurgent form – will see faith as first and foremost the Catholic faith of the Church, in which each member shares by belonging and loyally obeying. The hierarchical view of Church structure coheres well, moreover, with the view of truth as a hierarchy of demonstration from fundamental principles. The priest is at once the representative of the hierarchy and the one who *applies* the principles of the Church to the moral life of the faithful. Hence a firm distinction between the teaching and the taught Church is retained, along with a clear distinction between Church and non-Church. Through its sacramental jurisdiction, the Church brings the world under the Kingdom of God by extending the Church's hierarchical reign.

• THE PROTESTANT will, on the contrary, see personal faith as the foundation of the corporate. Nevertheless the Protestant, like the Roman Catholic, is a foundationalist, seeking truth by building outwards and upwards from sure foundations; it is just that those foundations now lie, not in the teaching of the *magisterium*, but in something graspable by each individual for himself or herself, whether through Scripture, reason or conscience. The minister is primarily the communicator of that information, by which the individual may convert to faith: the stress in ministry is not on the sacramental and hierarchical but on the evangelistic and didactic. Once again, the distinction between Church and non-Church is strong, but it corresponds to a boundary between Christian and non-Christian, which is crossed at conversion.

• THE ANGLICAN will see faith not so much as the foundation we start from but as something that emerges in the context of the life of the Church. It emerges not from the top down, as with the Catholic organism, nor from the bottom up, as with the Protestant crystal, but from the middle out, fractally. In ministry, the characteristic stress is on the *pastoral* work of the priest, as listener as well as teacher; both preaching and sacramental work are seen in primarily pastoral terms.[13] Word and world interact, and the Church's task is to facilitate this dialogue, in which the world is brought into communion with God. To this end the Church has infinitely complex, fractal boundaries like the edge of a cloud, or like roots or blood vessels. In a cloud there are parts that are definitely 'inside' it and parts that are clearly 'outside', but the boundary between inside and outside is convoluted and ever-changing, so that you cannot always tell which is inside which. We note that blood vessels have the kind of boundary that maximizes the area whereby oxygen and nutrients can be brought to the body's cells, and waste products taken from them. The Church, in the Anglican perspective, needs the same intricately branched and convoluted structure, so as to diffuse as much as possible of God's love and goodness into the world, and to draw out and offer up as much of the world's goodness and loving response.[14]

Clearly these three approaches to the Church need be no more mutually exclusive than the different approaches to the body. As a *growing* body, the Church grows out of the faith of its members; where faith is lacking, so will growth be. As an *active* body, the Church relies on hierarchical structures of co-ordination and control, to receive perceptions from the world, evaluate them according to the standards of faith, and to proceed to direct and inform action accordingly. And as a *living* body the Church requires the sacraments that enable the faith of members to gel and self-organize into this structure of coherent action.

Moreover, it is the relatively elusive fractal process that allows the crystal to grow into an organism. Without the fractal, the crystal will be in tension with the organism. Each will tend to claim too much by subsuming those roles that only the fractal can perform. So Anglicanism has an essential contribution to make, beyond that of simply being a reconciling 'middle way'.

Thus, on the one hand the typical Roman Catholic (and Anglo-Catholic) mistake is to assume that those hierarchical features that are necessary to the co-ordinated action of the world-wide Church are the very same features that are necessary for the Church to grow into being at all. Hence the error that episcopacy is of the *esse*, the very being of the Church: something without which a church cannot be Church at all. Against this, mainstream Anglicanism need have no difficulty in recognizing non-Episcopal churches as real Churches. The Church does not *grow* in the same way as the way in which it is best co-ordinated and guided, down an episcopal pipeline of succession flowing from the apostles. The bishops lead the Church, but they do not (in their role as bishops) propagate it. Ordination orders the Church, but baptism builds it.[15] And just as there is no papal neurone in the brain through which nerve activity must pass before it becomes conscious, so there is no papal individual or institution through which beliefs must pass before they become the mind of the Church.

Authority in the Church is as diffuse and global, and yet as real as consciousness in the brain.

Conversely, the typical Protestant mistake is to reduce the faith of the Church to that of its members, and to deny the beautiful way in which fellowship can become communion, whereby in the ordered worship of each local congregation, the whole Catholic Church of all places and ages is wholly present, each member dancing to the tune of a faith that transcends what he or she may personally be able to grasp. The structures of episcopacy (uniting all peoples geographically) and apostolic succession (uniting all ages temporally) though not essential to the *esse*, the being, are very much part of the *bene esse*, the well-being, the abundance of life of the Church, precisely because they are what guarantee this world-wide communion, as distinct from merely local fellowship. Though not all churches need have these features unbroken in their past, as Christ's (embryonic?) body they all need to be growing towards them in the future, just as any human embryo will be growing towards a co-ordinated unity in which it can act with integrity.

Tradition and communion

So faith informs the Church through *koinonia*, communion in the Body. The Emmaus road story tells us clearly that the Word is kindled in the heart in the process of being expounded and passed on, in a sharing whose culmination is communion – the 'breaking of bread'. As soon as the moment of communion and recognition has arrived, it has passed;

there is no Word left there for the Church to possess and store up for itself as bare Scripture, or reflect on by means of a detached, uncommitted reason, outside of the event of communion itself (Luke 24:13–35).

We cannot build tabernacles where we can store the transfiguring glory of the Word while we are away not communing with him (Mark 9:5, Matt. 17:4 and Luke 9:33). The individual cannot possess the Word of God in the tabernacle of his heart, but only insofar as he is speaking and hearing that Word in the communion of the Church will the fire of that Word burn with a living flame in that holy of holies. Nor can any central magisterium possess that infallible Word merely to pass on down to the ranks of the faithful. The central authority – like any other Christian individual or body – knows the Word to the extent that it is manifestly dancing in tune with the consensus of the faithful. It is the truth as lived in communion – including that intercommunion with past ages which is tradition, 'handing on' – that informs and judges both the institution's and the individual's hold on the truth.

For the reasons we have already looked at, if the Church is the communion of the Word of God, it is inseparable from the Scriptures and the right use of reason. The Church could be defined as the Community or Body which is 'membered' by the 'remembering' of Scripture; while the Scriptures could be defined as the written expression of the Word that the Church has historically chosen to be the remembering of. The Church speaks the Word, but in the process the Church is also spoken by the Word.

The Church is the Word re-enfleshing itself in human life, as human life re-members itself in the Word.

What this means is that the fraught search for the Word somehow grounded in human certainty (whether personal or institutional) is a mistake. Our attempts to capture the Word must give way to the Word that we allow to speak to us. And that is only heard and known in the *process by* which the participative life of the Church is maintained.

Summary

We are used to speaking of the Church as the Body of Christ, but just as there are different ways of understanding how the various parts of the body relate to the whole, there are different ways of viewing the relationship of individual Christians to the whole Church. The dominant Roman Catholic view sees the Body of Christ as a supernatural *organism*, with the Papacy at its head, in which each part functions within a complete system that is co-ordinated from the top down. The Protestant view typically sees the Church as a *crystalline* structure. Here the faith of each individual is primary, authority is derived from the bottom up, and the whole tends to be seen as the sum of its constituent parts. The Anglican, and perhaps Eastern Orthodox, view is typically *fractal*. This means that rather as consciousnes in the human body cannot be located in a specific part but 'emerges' in the body as a whole, in the Anglican Church faith or authority are derived not from the bottom up or the top down, but emerge from the lived experience of the communion of the Church.

Because of this dispersed nature of authority, the

boundaries of the Body are less clear-cut, facilitating the interaction of the Word and the world. As in the human body, 'organic' co-ordination and hierarchy are still required for united action, and the Church depends on the 'crystalline' growth of the Body through the conversion and commitment of each individual. But the exclusivity of these functions is denied. Thus, for example, the Anglican view of episcopacy is not that without it there can be no Church, but that it serves the well-being of the Church by focussing in the bishops an authority that belongs to the whole Body. The 'living Word' belongs not in any fixed tradition or hierarchical part of the Body to be handed down to the rest, but always relates to the whole. A hierarchy is needed in the Body, but it will be truly authoritative only insofar as it is in tune with the consensus of all the Body's members. Similarly with regard to Scripture; Scripture is in a sense the Church's creation (since the Church, moved by the living Word, determined its contents). But at the same time the Church is also created and informed by Scripture as it continues to respond to the Word speaking through it. Once again it is hearing the living Word that matters, as it comes to us through the interactive process of being in communion with the life of the Church.

Reason: Contemplative Imagination

Historically, biblicism and rationalism have sometimes managed to be temporary bedfellows. They have been able to collaborate in their attack on the mystery or the mystification of the Church. They share a desire to pare away unnecessary accretions and lay bare good, honest, simple foundations. But biblicists are prepared to stop short at (biblical) fundamentals, whereas the more radical 'fundamentalism' of pure rationalism goes on to challenge that even these foundations are not fundamental enough. There the happy relationship ends. Once the lived interpretation that *is* the Church has been pared away, biblicism and rationalism part, and shatter themselves in turn into innumerable rival sects or schools.

But it is only the characteristically modern 'foundationalist', sceptical use of reason that is necessarily the enemy, first of the Church, then of the Bible. More ancient Platonic, and more recent 'postmodern' understandings of reason call into question this whole sceptical enterprise, and link reason with contemplation or imagination: the Platonic contemplation of eternal truth, or the postmodern imagination of story and its embodiment in forms of life. Both link reason with a poetic strand that has never been lost in Anglicanism, from the poetry of Cranmer's liturgy, through Richard Hooker and his corporate and cosmic *logos*,[16] the Metaphysical poets, the Cambridge Platonists, Coleridge, the Romantic aspect of the Oxford Movement and the Ritualists, to T. S. Eliot and R. S. Thomas. For its size, Anglicanism is remarkable for the quality and quantity of its religious verse, though it is strange how little Anglican theologians have attended to this resource.

Contemplative imagination can still do some of the work of scepticism. For integral to contemplation is the *via negativa*, the negative way of prayer into the bright darkness of God that shatters our idolatrous images till we are left with a naked and purified attention. But the goal is different. Scepticism seeks a self-possessed certainty, based on our own rational resources, whereas the *via negativa* seeks the loving embrace of a dispossessed faith, falling into the hands of the living God. And because neither we nor any creature can be self-possessed and self-sustaining, scepticism ends in nihilism and nothingness, whereas mystical prayer ends by falling into the infinite abyss that is the embrace of the everlasting arms.

It is, I contend, precisely this contemplative understanding of reason that makes some of the disputes between Scripture, reason and tradition so baffling to mainstream Anglicans. For this is an imaginative, story-telling, vision-forming kind of reason, well equipped for the prophetic *anamnesis* (remembrance in the sense of making present, as in the Eucharist) of biblical story through tradition and on into new world-visions. It is arguably, too, just such a reason that is appropriate to faith. Precisely because its aim is certainty and proof, sceptical reason is hostile to faith, which involves risking the unproven. Imaginative reason on the other hand will by nature grope outwards (the process the Greek Fathers called *epektasis*) towards that vision in the darkness that is essential to faith, and to the living of Scripture and tradition in prayer.

Perhaps an analogy with our personal growth is appropriate here. Our adult life is a creative retelling of our childhood story. Much of that story lies buried and forgotten, but in our adult life we re-member it as we live. We live, indeed, by the interaction, aided and moulded by the reasoning imagination, between our childhood and our present. We may become prisoners of our past, of course, merely repeating outworn patterns. In the same way we can be slaves to the Scriptures or tradition. Or with equal neurosis we can repress our past and become slaves to the present. Only by an ever-wider retelling of our story, assimilating broader tracts of experience, do we grow healthily. Thus the issue of women priests hinges on whether it involves (as some say) a forgetting, an unhealthy repression, of the priestly 'story', or (as I argue) a wider retelling of it, assimilating to it that feminine experience that was hitherto repressed. At its best the Anglican triad shows the way to a liberating and un-neurotic growth in the Church.

Summary

What rationalism (basing itself on human reason alone) and biblicism (basing itself on Scripture alone) have in common is the misplaced drive to pare away the *lived* interpretation of the Word in the communion of the Church in order to reach some concrete, objective foundation for faith. With regard to reason, however, this modern, 'fundamentalist' view is not the only one possible. Both ancient philosophy (especially Platonism) and a 'postmodern' approach enlarge the concept of reason to include mysticism and the imagination. Whereas sceptical rationalism seeks an isolated, self-possessed certainty based on our own resources – and so is liable to end in nothingness and despair – the reasoning of contemplative imagination accepts that no objective, self-possessed grasp of reality is obtainable, and instead is open to seeking truth through *being possessed by* reality by way of the imagination, poetry, contemplation, and prayer. Whereas sceptical rationalism strives vainly after objective, graspable proofs, faith by definition accepts that truth ultimately lies in reaching out through darkness and uncertainty to that which lies beyond.

This kind of imaginitive reasoning is as crucial to the Church as to a growing person. As adults we are constantly remoulding and recreating the patterns of our personality that we received from our childhood, as we assimilate new knowledge and experience. Without this function of the reasoning imagination we would either remain childish, the prisoner of outworn patterns; or alternatively we might cut away our personal roots in the past and become superficial slaves of the present, out of touch with our deeper selves. Healthy growth depends on reflective and creative interaction between past and present experience. Similarly in the Church we will be equally stunted if we are slaves to Scripture or tradition, or if we forget them entirely and are slaves to present and passing fashion. 'Imaginative reasoning' makes the link between Scripture, tradition and our present experience, and that is the way we grow.

Prospects

To return to our opening analogy, the compass of reason is useless without a map. The compass alone can tell us where North is, and where South, but without a map we cannot tell which way is worth going. So undiluted rationalism leaves us in a moral void. But maps alone are useless too; we cannot place ourselves on them, or relate them to the landscape we know. For this, we need the compass of imaginative reason, which enables us to place our space in biblical space, and allows the Bible's unexplained ciphers to become landmarks for our present. But even when we have learnt where we are on the map there is still the process of deciding where now to go, which ways will be easy, which tough, which rewarding; and for that we need to learn from those who have walked here before us and have experience to share and pool within the co-ordinated communion of the Church.

If the Church is a communion in which diverse parts function in one whole, we do not need to seek the probably impossible ideal whereby every member would accept the triad and work with it personally; nor do we need to set up a magisterium to arbitrate and make final decisions for faith on the basis of the triad. There will still be room in the Anglican *koinonia* for biblical fundamentalists, authoritarian Catholics, and radical sceptics; they may even have an integral role in ensuring that none of the triad is underestimated.

These positions need to be retained within the sacramental and theological *koinonia* of the Church. But that does need to be a *koinonia* of faith and vision, not a solely sacramental communion of people determined to keep their ideas separated by impermeable walls! To this end, the following suggestions emerge.

1. THE DIALOGUE AND EXCHANGE BETWEEN THE THREE EXTREME STANDPOINTS. This needs to be strengthened at all costs, and it has a double implication for ministerial training. It is necessary to preserve the distinctness of the three main traditions, but also to facilitate their interaction. It is important to have colleges, and moreover, to develop courses, that have a distinct churchmanship, but this strong distinctiveness needs to be seen as a necessity for the good of the whole, not as something self-sufficient and as being in some sense the only authentic form of Anglicanism, let alone Christianity. Evangelical colleges and courses need to ensure, for example, that they have Catholic and Liberal members of staff and placement parishes, and close relations with Roman Catholic and Orthodox churches, while retaining, even developing, their Evangelical spirituality and stress on Scripture. Liberal and Catholic colleges and courses need to make corresponding adjustments. And diocesan direc-

tors of lay training need to ensure both that the distinctive traditions are full-bloodedly represented in training courses, and that they interact creatively.

2. THE ANGLICAN HEARTLAND NEEDS RENEWING. The old liberal 'centre' could not hold the extremes together: because it was in fact not a centre but a third extreme as hostile to Catholic and Evangelical as they were to each other! I imagine the most promising way for a strong, vibrant centre to come about is through a creative interaction between Affirming Catholics and Open Evangelicals. Each is fired by a distinctive spirituality while being 'liberal' in the broad sense of being receptive to the other's tradition, and broadly affirmative of the threefold way outlined in this book. To some extent such a dialogue has begun to happen; it is certainly what lies behind the splendid liturgical creativity of the recent Church of England. If what I have argued is true, it is the coming together of these particular movements that holds the key to the Church of England's future insofar as it has one: that is, the key to this Church's ability to move forward in a coherent way.

3. FRACTAL INSTITUTIONAL STRUCTURES. So that the Anglican theology of dialogue (or 'trialogue') may be sustained, we need to develop fractal institutional structures – something like a Christian university, perhaps – in every diocese or region. The Cathedrals might even recover a *raison d'etre* as the basis of such 'worshipping universities'. These universities would act as a focus for a far wider, more diffused, fractal

network of idea exchange than current theology faculties and theological colleges provide. At present, an elite of professional theologians practise a theology that tends, by the nature of the academic context, towards the rationalist and sceptical. Meanwhile professional clerics theologize Sunday by Sunday in the preaching of the Word, but in a manner that often bears little sign of leavening by the insights and discoveries of academic theology, and in many quarters seems magnetically attracted to the biblicist pole. And finally we witness a deepening demand for 'spirituality' and the burgeoning of books and poems that explore the depths of the soul, but sometimes draw more from secular psychology than theology.

This is but another aspect of the fragmentation of the triad. Our academic, prophetic and mystical theologies need, for their own good and the good of the Church as a whole, to be drawn into creative interaction. This requires a networking between some very diverse groups, not all of which need themselves to be explicitly Christian: academic theologians, providing intellectual rigour and expertise; what one might term practical theologians, reflective clergy and laity engaged at the coal-face of Christian action in society, sharpening theological tools through their praxis; mystical theologians, that is, communities of believers engaged in the discovery of God through prayer (which is why the university would need to be a *worshipping* university); symbolic theologians, poets and artists, struggling to give material embodiment to the life of the spirit in the current age; and inter-faith theologians, discovering more of the Christian God through interaction with other traditions of belief; to name but a few! If theology unfolds through the interaction between scriptural revelation, symbolically embodied tradition, and the rational imagination, then it is not so much within these separate disciplines that theology is likely to happen, but in the disciplined interaction between them.

4. THE 'TURNBULL REPORT'. At the time of writing I have not read this report of the *The Archbishops' Commission on the Organization of the Church of England*[17] – but the introductory leaflet made me wonder. We certainly need to ensure that, as an organism, the Church of England is well-organized and efficient. But we have seen that the Church as a body organized for action needs to be held in tension with the Church as a crystal growing around God's Word, and the Church as a fractal network loosely focused on Holy Communion. Unless, in the debate about to begin, these other vital aspects are borne in mind, the beautiful threefold balance of the Church of England could easily be thrown out of kilter. The result would be a Romanizing zeal for efficient hierarchical control, which in the absence of the Roman Catholic Church's reverence for the constraints of tradition, would make for a godless, self-managing Church; or to put it apocalyptically, 'the abomination of desolation'.

5. WAYS TOWARDS A SPIRITUAL SEA-CHANGE. Of course, all the above require a spiritual sea-change, such that we accept that our traditions are not the treasure but the earthen vessels containing it. We all need to use the rich resources we already have with a postmodern humility – not craving to be right, or certain, but willing to learn, and willing to adventure by faith – and also systematically, with the discipline, logic, and vision of poets of the scriptural, cosmic and incarnate Word. Then we may begin to find our way, not just for ourselves or even the wider Church, but – because the agenda of reconciling religious traditions with secular modernity is an urgent global one – for the whole of humanity.

6. RESTORING OUR CONFIDENCE. Finally, within this humility – because I hope I have have made it obvious that there are no grounds for Anglican complacency – I would also hope that this booklet might do something to restore the confidence of the beleaguered Anglican church! Chastened by our diminishing wealth, power and influence, by the internal divisions that threaten our integrity as a communion, and not least, by a frequently bad press that majors on scandals, we have reason to be humble. But if what I have written has any truth at all, and if we can begin to act positively using the interdependence of our rich diversities in the coherent way I suggest, rather than as a melée of competing sub-sects, then we will also have cause to be as the title of Stephen Sykes' recent book urges, 'unashamed Anglicans'.

Summary

Ideally the triad of Scripture, tradition and reason operates within each individual Christian, but more importantly it operates as a function of the communion of the Church, within which different individuals and groups will naturally emphasize one or another element in the triad. It is crucial for the Church's health and growth that dialogue between the three standpoints is encouraged. Catholic, Evangelical and Liberal groups must understand themselves not as sub-sects, preserving the one 'authentic' form of Anglicanism, but as called to offer their distinctive insight to the whole.

Theological colleges in particular need to show openness to traditions other than their own; and there is great scope for creative interaction and co-operation between particular churchmanship groups. We need centres to promote theological work that is different from the self-contained, sceptical–rationalist kind of theology which dominates University theology faculties; and we need theologians who are open to pastoral, mystical and inter-faith insights. In the forthcoming reorganizing of the Church of England it will be important that concern for 'working as one body' does not lead to an organic, quasi-Roman kind of hierarchical control which might upset the balance of the Anglican 'trialogue'. Above all, as groups and individuals we need both a new humility and a new confidence: humility to learn from traditions other than our own, and confidence in Anglicanism itself and the rich potential of its unique approach.

Questions

Introduction

1. Is the author's allegory of the map game a good one for the present state of the Anglican Church? How fair is his depiction of the different parties involved in it?

2. Is your own inclination to place greatest authority on Scripture, tradition or reason? Why?

3. What distinction is the author drawing between fundamentalism and what he calls 'foundationalism'? Why does he think both are unsatisfactory?

4. Do you agree that absolute certainty and infallible authority are unattainable in this life?

5. How do you set about making up your mind on current questions about women's ordination, gay relationships, abortion, remarriage after divorce, surrogate parenting and so on? What does this say about where authority really lies for you?

Scripture: The Inbreathed Word

1. How much difference would there be in practice between what the author calls the 'biblicist' and 'fun-

damentalist' approaches to Scripture – for example in their understanding of the creation stories in Genesis?

2. What is the difference between these approaches and the approach suggested by the Articles of The Book of Common Prayer?

3. Why do you think the biblicist or fundamentalist approach is so popular in the Church today?

4. How would you explain to a new Christian what is meant by the 'word of God', specially in relation to Scripture?

5. Do you agree with this author that (for Anglicans) the Bible is 'less a book to be read than to be breathed, proclaimed and sung?' What are the risks in this approach?

6. Do you feel you know much about the Bible, and that you understand it when you hear or read it? Do you feel it matters?

Church: Organism, Assembly and Communion

1. Do you find the author's illustration of the 'organic' 'crystalline' and 'fractal' views of the body helpful? How far do you think it illuminates real differences in Roman Catholic, Protestant and Anglican approaches?

2. Bishop Turnbull has described the decision-making structures in the Church of England as resembling 'a dismembered jellyfish'. How dispersed is dispersed authority in our Church, and is it a good thing?

3. The author thinks the 'fractal' character of the Anglican Church facilitates interaction between the Word and the world. Is it true? Where is the evidence?

4. Are the blurred boundaries of the Church of England more to do with Establishment than with Anglicanism's 'fractal' character as described here? Do you know (or can you imagine) the experience of other provinces in the Anglican Communion, where Anglicans are a tiny minority?

5. How blurred should the Church's boundaries be? Is there a good and a bad sort of blurring?

6. Should bishops be more than a focus of consensus in the Church? What do you think is the proper role and authority of a bishop?

Reason: Contemplative Imagination
1. Do you agree that one can be just as 'fundamentalist' about human reason as about Scripture? Can you think of any examples?

2. Why do you think theologians have generally been uninterested in religious poetry and other imaginative or devotional expressions of faith? Do you agree that this is a mistake?

3. The author refers to the *via negativa*: the view that through growth in prayer our personal images and ideas about God are progressively shattered and shed, until in the end we learn to stop trying to picture or 'possess' God mentally, but rather are possessed by

him. Does this fit in with any of your experience of praying and growing in faith?

4. How do you understand the word *faith*? Do you agree that faith itself means 'risking the unproven'? What is the basis of your faith?

5. The author thinks that healthy growth for a person and for a church depends on creatively reconciling past and present experience. Do you think the Church is too much stuck in the past and so failing to relate properly to the present, or is it too much forgetting its past (the Scriptures and tradition) and getting carried away with present trends? Or is it doing both in different areas?

Prospects
1. How does the triad of Scripture, reason and tradition operate within the individual Christian? How do you use and balance these resources in your own spiritual life and growth?

2. Do you agree that the Church may still need its 'fundamentalists' of all three persuasions?

3. What could you or your church do to facilitate exchange and discussion with Anglicans of a different churchmanship?

4. Why does the author describe the Anglican Church as 'beleaguered'? What do you see as the best way to recapture confidence?

5. What denomination would you join if you were

not an Anglican, and why? What do you see as the advantages of Anglicanism?

Notes and References

1. Cf. *Laws of Ecclesiastical Polity* III. viii. 13–15.

2. Aidan Nichols, *The Panther and the Hind*, T. & T. Clark, 1993.

3. In *The Integrity of Anglicanism* (London, Mowbray, 1978) p.33, Stephen Sykes argues that liberalism cannot be reckoned as a centrist party between the Catholics and Evangelicals.

4. For more on foundationalism, see my 'Scientific and religious understanding' (*The Way*, October 1992) pp.258ff. In *Holy Ground*, London, SPCK, 1991, I follow Polanyi's line, that we can have non-provable knowledge of real objects, the knowledge we have of persons being a case in point. This is crucial for the present discussion.

5. Henry Vaughan, *The Night*.

6. On this process of retelling, cf. Gerard Loughlin, 'Writing the Trinity,' *Theology*, London, SPCK, March 1994.

7. For the concept of re-membering I am indebted to David Moss, 'Re-membering Baptism' (*Theology*, London, SPCK, March 1994).

8. The concept of a fractal was introduced and beautifully illustrated by Bénoît Mandelbrot in *The Fractal Geometry of Nature*, Freeman, 1982. On self-organizing 'dissipative structures' in nature, cf. Ilya Prygogine and Isabelle Stengers, *Order out of Chaos*, Fontana, 1985. Easy introductions may be found in the writings of Paul Davies, James Gleick, William Poundstone and others, and in Chapter 7 of my own *Holy Ground* (op.cit.).

9. Cf. Daniel C. Dennett, *Consciousness Explained*, London, Penguin, 1991; also Marvin Minsky, *The Society of Mind*, Simon and Schuster, 1985.

10. On *koinonia* as constitutive of the Church cf. John Zizioulas, *Being as Communion*, St Vladimir's Seminary Press, 1993, worth comparing with my notion of *diousia* or a dialogue of being as constitutive of being itself, in *Holy Ground*.

11. Cf. William Crockett, 'Holy Communion', in *Anglican Studies* (London, SPCK, 1988), esp. p.274 on Hooker.

12. Cf. Stephen Sykes, 'Cranmer on the Open Heart,' in *Unashamed Anglicanism* (London, Darton, Longman & Todd, 1995), pp.24ff.

13. Conversely, pastoral care is a wider concept in Anglicanism than simply helping the needy. Cf. O. C. Edwards, 'Anglican pastoral tradition', in *Anglican Studies* (op.cit.).

14. Robin Gill has shown in his *The Myth of the Empty Church*, London, SPCK, 1993, the Anglican tendency to want a church presence, however small, in every community, is not a strategy for growth in total membership; but the issue of which matters most, total membership or dispersed presence, is one I would obviously wish to debate.

15. Stephen Sykes argues that baptism is thus fundamental in 'Foundations of an Anglican Ecclesiology,' in *Unashamed Anglicanism* (op.cit.) pp.122ff. I agree with this in part.

16. Cf. A. S. McGrade, 'Reason,' in *Anglican Studies* (op.cit.), p.108.

17. Church House, 1995.